101 THINGS TO DO BEFORE SECONDARY SCHOOL

Louise Spilsbury

D1102671

CONTENTS

Read All About It!   2

Squeeze a Year into a Book   4

Go Away!   6

Become a Star   8

Sit on Stress   10

Speak Without Words!   12

Win an Award   14

Leave With a Laugh   16

Show You Care!   18

Take the Tourist Challenge   20

Perfect a Party Trick   22

Customise Your Kit   24

Be Prepared!   26

Survive Your First Day   28

Enjoy It!   30

Glossary and Index   32

READ ALL ABOUT iT!

How am I going to make the most of my year?

Doesn't time fly? Can you believe it's only a year until you go to secondary school? It may seem like a long time but you'll be surprised how quickly it goes. So what are you going to do to make it a year to remember? No idea? Well, don't worry – that's what this book is for!

How can this book help?

In this book you'll find 101 amazing things to try, make and do in your last year at primary school. Want to make your leavers' day the best ever? Or wow your friends with some tricky tricks? We'll show you how! What about your last summer holiday before secondary school? What are you going to do to make it special? We have some ace ideas. Worried about your first day at secondary? Then you need our survival tips.

Just do it!

Sounds simple, doesn't it? But hang on, what do *you* need to do? Well 101 activities is actually quite a lot to do in one year. Let's get practical. You won't be able to do everything at once so you need to decide exactly what you *are* going to do and when.

1 Top five
Look through the book, and choose the top five things you most want to do.

How will I get ready for secondary school?

FAST FACT

Kimani Nganga Maruge is proof that you're never too old to take on a challenge. In 2004 Mr Maruge became the oldest person in the world to start primary school. He had to wait until he was 84 because Kenya only introduced free schooling in 2003 and he couldn't afford to go before then!

Top Tip!

This is no ordinary book. It's really quite clever. Each new page looks at something different. That means you can start wherever you want.

Are you still here? Go on – turn the page and find something fun to do!

2 SQUEEZE A YEAR INTO A BOOK

A year in a book? How's that possible? Simple – all you have to do is make your very own yearbook.

My Year Squished Flat in a Book

Our trip to Number 10

Date: Monday 14th March

No one ever dreamed this day would come but, on a cold morning in March, we set out for the capital to claim our prize. After winning the Green Challenge, we were going to Number 10 to meet the Prime Minister. I was very nervous as I had been chosen to talk to him but he was really nice and we talked for ages. We even had our picture taken. It was an amazing day.

The door at Number 10 can only be opened from the inside.

Question and answer corner

	Josh	Abi
What will you miss most?	I'll miss school dinners. I love Mrs M's cottage pie ... mmmmm!	You of course – you're my best friend!
What's the funniest thing that happened to you?	I forgot my lines for the school play but made something up that was even funnier.	When I got the giggles in class and Miss Walker started laughing and couldn't stop!

Write about school trips, important events and funny stories.

FAST FACT
Yearbooks record the last year of school. They've been around for years, especially in the USA where the first one was published in 1806.

Ask friends to answer funny questions in your book.

Take photos of your friends and ask them to write something about you.

My friends

Name: Abi
Age: 10³/₄

I've known Mary since our first day at primary school. She's so kind and she always makes me laugh. I hope we stay friends forever.

Name: Josh Akram
Age: 10

I met Mary when I moved schools. I was so nervous on my first day but Mary made me feel right at home.

South Oakwood Lift Cup

South Oakwood's football team were triumphant yesterday after winning the South Schools' Cup. Team captain Martin James said, "We played as a team and that's why we've won!"

Include reports about school clubs and sports days.

3 ## Forget me not

Design and make an **autograph** book. Get everyone to sign it and write a special message. You never know – one day one of them might be famous!

4 ## Wear it with pride!

Persuade everyone to sign your T-shirt, but ask permission from home first!

5 ## Get digging

Fill a **time capsule** with things that relate to your last year at primary school. Who knows who will find it in the future?

6 ## Make sweet music

Choose a special song and record the whole class singing it.

7 ## Make it news

Compose a class newsletter – think of a catchy headline!

8 ## Let it grow

Plant a class tree and be remembered long after you leave school.

Get snap happy with a camera on ideas 16 and 61. These will make essential viewing for your yearbook. Say cheese!

9 GO AWAY!

It's good to escape the classroom every now and again. Whether for a study trip or just for fun, you're bound to learn something new. Even if the rain pours down, which let's face it, it probably will, you'll still enjoy every minute. So, go on – go away!

Do what?

Teachers work hard all year, so why not help them to plan a school trip? First talk to your teacher. Use your sweetest smile, politest voice and most persuasive tone to ask them if you can help to organise the trip. If they agree to that, you need to get the rest of the class to agree on where to go!

Things to do

- If it is too tricky to get everyone to agree on a trip, vote on it.
- Look on the internet to find out more about places to visit.
- Decide whether the trip will be during school or after school.
- Research how much the trip will cost.
- Decide on your means of transport.
- Make a poster to advertise the trip to persuade lots of people to come!

FAST FACT
Schools can only ask for a voluntary contribution for school trips. That means parents or carers pay what they can afford to.

10 Go large
I'd like to go on a trip to a giant cinema to see a 3D film. Something scary!

Mary Macnaghten

11 Take a ride!
What about a trip to a theme park or an adventure park? I love rollercoasters!

Alex Warden

12 Park life
I think we should definitely go on a walk in the countryside. We could have a picnic, play games and learn about the wildlife in the area.

Caroline Phipps

Top Tip!

Remember to discuss everything with your teachers first. They are the ones who really organise everything, so work with them. Use your best persuasive skills and don't forget to listen to what they have to say.

Where would you most like to go on a school trip?

THE GREAT ESCAPE

FANCY ESCAPING SCHOOL FOR A DAY?

THIS YEAR WE, THE PUPILS, ARE HELPING TO ORGANISE THE SCHOOL TRIP.

TOGETHER WE CAN MAKE IT THE BEST EVER!

WHERE DO YOU THINK WE SHOULD GO?

HOW ABOUT SWIMMING, SIGHTSEEING OR SURFING?

THERE ARE SO MANY EXCELLENT CHOICES!

ALL IDEAS NEED TO BE IN BEFORE 20TH APRIL.

13 Strike it lucky
My top choice would be to go to score some pins at an indoor bowling alley.
Josh Ward

14 Get hands on
If it's a school trip, we should go to a museum and learn something new. How about a science museum?
Sarah Dale

15 Surf's up
Let's do some fundraising and go away for a residential trip, like a week by the seaside.
Ali Patel

16 BECOME A STAR

Have you ever dreamed of becoming a star? Treading the boards on stage and being adored by your army of fans? Well, now's your chance! Almost every school in the country puts on a show or a play at the end of Year 6. Win a starring role and wow the audience!

Show off!

Most schools hold **auditions**. It's your chance to shine, but an audition can also be quite scary. Here are some suggestions for attracting the **director's** attention.

1. Choose a song, poem or part of a play for your audition piece, but keep it to about 2 minutes long.

2. Rehearse your piece until it is word perfect.

3. Just before the audition, practise some tongue twisters to loosen up your voice.

4. At the audition, hold your head up, look confident and speak loudly, slowly and clearly.

5. If you think you fluffed it, ask permission to do it again.

Become like the **paparazzi** and take photos for idea 2!

You might feel nervous auditioning for a show, but you'll feel better and perform better if you're well prepared.

17 Get practising
Learn five songs off by heart that you can sing really well for any audition.

18 Steal the show
Rehearse a song and dance to give the school show a grand finale.

19 Spread your wings
Don't stop once the show is over. Join a local drama company.

20 Test your talent
To become a star you have to be noticed, so enter a talent show.

21 Do a bit of DIY
Do-It-Yourself! Persuade your friends to help you write and produce your own play.

22 Change your name!
Plan your **stage name** for the future – what would you like to see up in lights?

FAST FACT
Some school stars do become famous. Daniel Radcliffe, lead actor in the Harry Potter films, began acting at the age of six when he appeared as a monkey in a school play!

23 SiT ON STRESS

Year 6 can be a lot of fun. Especially when you have 101 new things to try, make and do! But what if things start to weigh you down, like lots of school work or tests? Your last year can be a very busy time, so how can you make sure you don't let things get on top of you?

Under pressure

Firstly, don't worry too much. Small amounts of stress can be good. If you never felt stress or excitement, life would be very dull! And when you feel under a bit of pressure, you often work harder and do better. Stress only becomes a problem when you become too anxious. Then you can feel tired, miserable or even ill.

Work it out!

To sit on stress, don't sit! Stand, walk, jump, run! Exercise is a great stress-buster. But don't try bouncing around in class – your teacher wouldn't appreciate that! Instead, make the most of playtime. Run around outside and get your heart racing. When you go back to class you'll feel so much better and you'll even be able to concentrate better on your work.

Top Tip!
Don't just exercise at playtime – make the most of games lessons and exercise after school and at weekends. Playing sport is a great way to take your mind off your worries too.

FAST FACT
Exercise makes you hot, but it also makes you chilled! After a workout your body releases chemicals that make you feel relaxed and happy.

24 Walk the dog

Earn bonus points with the family and get some exercise at the same time by walking the dog. No dog? Just take a parent out for some fresh air instead!

25 On your bike!

Cycling is a great way to exercise, especially when you do it with friends. Remember to stay safe – wear a helmet and let someone know where you are going.

26 Make a graph

Sometimes it's hard to know when you're most stressed. Make a happiness chart to record your feelings for a week. Does this show you when you feel stressed? Could you do anything to change this?

27 Be positive

Don't beat yourself up about what you haven't done. Be proud of what you have done.

28 Do nothing

Take breaks when you're doing homework. The brain sucks up a fifth of your energy, so downtime is good.

29 Make learning fun

Use colours, silly rhymes and pictures to help you remember facts when revising for tests.

30 Get your five a day

Eating at least five portions of fruit and vegetables a day helps to keep you healthy.

31 Spread the load

Do some homework every day. That way it won't pile up and start to worry you.

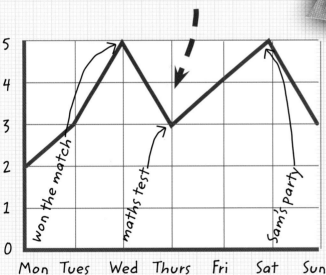

How do you feel when you know you have a lot of work to do?

SPEAK WITHOUT WORDS!

One thing you might get stressed about is visiting your future secondary school. There may be so many questions buzzing round in your head. What will the other students be like? Will they like you? Will you look shy and nervous?

Keep your mouth shut

If you learn about body language, you'll be able to tell people you're a nice, friendly kind of person without even opening your mouth!

Body talk

Talking is just one way to **communicate**. People also use a lot of **postures** and **gestures** to express their feelings. When you meet a friend in the street you show you are happy to see them by smiling and waving. Can you read other people's body language?

FAST FACT
At least 70 per cent of human communication is non-verbal. That means people say more in the way they stand, hold their arms and the different expressions on their face than they ever say in words!

When you frown and look away or look at someone with your eyes narrowed you look unfriendly.

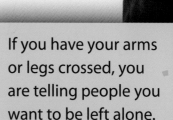

If you have your arms or legs crossed, you are telling people you want to be left alone.

What does your body language say about you?

Top Tip!

When you talk to someone, hold your head up, look at them and speak clearly and naturally. That way you'll seem friendly and confident – even if you don't feel it!

Making eye contact when you're talking to someone will suggest you are friendly and taking notice of what they are saying.

To appear welcoming and friendly uncross your arms and smile.

33 Look into my eyes

Practise smiling with your eyes. Sounds strange? Give it a go. Look in the mirror and try to make your eyes smile. Smiling eyes show that you're friendly.

34 Learn mirroring

Practise copying someone else's body language – it makes them relax and suggests you are friendly. Don't try too hard though or they might think you're making fun of them.

35 Get chatting

Learn five attention-grabbing questions you can ask different people to start a conversation.

36 Listen up!

Practise listening carefully to what people say. Ask them questions about what they say and they will feel like you're really interested.

37 Keep it simple

It sounds simple but don't forget to say 'hello'. Introduce yourself to as many people in your new class as you can – and try to remember all their names!

38 Make them an offer

Offer to eat lunch or go out to break with someone. They are probably feeling nervous too.

13

39 WIN AN AWARD

Before heading off to secondary school, take time to appreciate the people at primary school. Your classmates are special so why not have a class awards day to reward everyone's skills and talents? Don't forget your teacher probably deserves an award too!

And the winner is ...

Your awards should be for the things that really make each person in your class unique. Who tells the best jokes? Who is always helpful? Who works really hard? You could put a list of class names on a board and ask for (kind) suggestions of what each person should win an award for. Here are some you could copy.

Best Time Keeper
CONGRATULATIONS
You have only been late 3 times this year!

Funniest Classmate
CONGRATULATIONS
You've had us rolling on the floor with laughter all year!

Best Smile of the Year
CONGRATULATIONS
Your happy smile cheers us all up!

Don't forget to add your award to your yearbook. See idea 2.

Top Tip!
Awards ceremonies should be fun. You don't want anyone feeling hurt or embarrassed on the big day, so make sure you only give out awards that people will be happy with.

Best Dancer
CONGRATULATIONS
You pull some great shapes! Keep moving!

Best Teacher
CONGRATULATIONS
You've made it through a year with us!

40 Roll out the red carpet

The Oscars are the most famous film awards in the world. Why not borrow a red carpet for the winners to walk down and ask everyone to dress up in their fanciest gear?

41 Beat your parents

Organise a parent-pupil football match. The losers could make or buy a cake for the winners as a prize!

42 Guess who?

Get teachers to bring in their old school photos and see if you can guess who's who.

43 Fingers on the buzzer

Make up a quiz and divide the class into teams. What will the winning team get?

44 Be a record breaker

Get a real award! Get your school involved in a World Record attempt, like making the longest ever line of socks!

45 Get wacky

Award prizes for some wacky races on silly things like space-hoppers, roller skates or tricycles!

46 Be board, not bored!

Organise a board games day at school – the winning team could win a board game!

FACT FILE

Here are some record breaking attempts to inspire you:

- The most mince pies eaten in a minute: 2 (It's harder than it sounds!)
- The largest piggy back race in the world: 296 participants ran a 100m race in just 2 minutes and 5 seconds in total
- The largest photo album in the world: measures 6.27m in height and 4.54m in width.

Don't cry! OK, maybe just a few tears because we all know leavers' assemblies can be sad. It's hard saying goodbye to people you've known for a long time but why not lighten the mood and have some fun? There's nothing like a few laughs to make a memorable day.

Top Tip!
Jokes are only funny if they don't hurt people's feelings.

Fill it with fun

One way to fill your leavers' day with laughter is to learn some great jokes and have a stand-up routine as part of the assembly. You could also scan in photos of some of the funniest things that have happened in your class over the year and project them onto a screen for all to see. Class members could take turns telling the hilarious stories behind the photos.

Only joking!

What's the secret of a good joke? Make it topical. Find jokes that suit the occasion. If it's a school leavers' day, research lots of jokes about schools, teachers and homework.

Here are some to get you started …

Can you tell me what the outer part of a tree is called?

Bark, boy, bark!

Q: What kind of tree does a maths teacher climb?
A: Geometry!

Q: Why was the maths book unhappy?
A: It had too many problems!

Q: What school subject are snakes best at?
A: Hissstory!

Think back to idea 9 – any funny stories to tell from your school trip?

The cost of teacher's presents

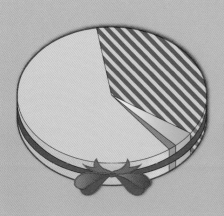

Under £5:	57.8%
£5–10	37.0%
£11–15	3.8%
Over £20	1.3%

This pie chart shows how much money people spend on presents for their teachers.

FACT FILE

The top five gifts that pupils give to teachers are:
1. chocolates
2. flowers and plants
3. wine
4. toiletries
5. mugs.

I don't know, Sir.

OK, Sir. "Woof! Woof!"

48 Be soppy
You don't have to buy your teacher a present to say thank you. Think of something different to do, like make them a special card or write them a poem.

49 Plan a party
Have an afternoon party and invite all the teachers, catering staff and anyone else who has helped your class.

50 Switch roles
Get the teachers to dress as pupils and the pupils as teachers for the day.

51 Pull some shapes
Organise a disco, decorate the school hall with lights, find a DJ with some banging tunes and bust some moves on the dance floor.

52 Get singing
Select a leavers' song that you can all sing, perhaps a song about friendship?

53 Imagine the future!
Write a class play about a school reunion in 20 years' time. What do you think you'll all be doing?

54 SHOW YOU CARE!

No one wants to lose touch with old mates when they leave primary school. One way to cement a friendship is by making friendship bracelets together. Show you care – why not make a matching pair and wear one each?

How to do it

These may look hard at first but once you've got the hang of it, they are really easy to do.

You will need:
- embroidery thread or wool
- sticky tape
- scissors

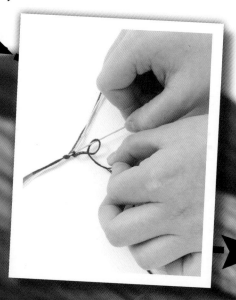

1
Choose four colours. Find colours that clash or colours that blend! Cut an arm's length of thread for each colour. Tie all the threads together in a knot at the top. Stick the knotted threads to a table.

2
Take the first thread on the left. Pull the second thread with your other hand really tightly. Wrap the first thread around the second to make a knot. Do this again. Then take the second thread and knot it around the third twice. Keep going like this with each thread.

3
Keep making the knots like this until the bracelet is long enough to go round your wrist.

Joining a sports club (see idea 56) is a great way to get exercise and exercise reduces stress – remember idea 23?

55 Club together

Join a club with friends, like Guides or Scouts. That way you'll meet up with them at least once a week!

56 Get sporty

Join a local sports team together. This will be good for you and good for your friendship!

57 Get creative

Write a poem about friendship to give to your best friend. It doesn't have to be too soppy – just tell them why their friendship is important to you.

58 Stay in

Plan to have a big night in watching films or playing games with friends once a fortnight. Don't forget the popcorn!

59 Speak in secret

Devise a secret code to communicate with your friends. That way when they write you a note, only you will be able to read it!

60 Stay in touch

How many different ways can you think of to say 'Hi' to your old friends? Phone them, send them photos or write them texts and emails.

4
Tie a knot in the other end and snip off any straggly ends. Now you're ready to tie the two ends together around your friend's wrist to make the bracelet!

FAST FACT
Friendship bracelets were first made by Native Americans. You should wear them until they break – removing them sooner is a sign the friendship has ended!

61 TAKE THE TOURIST CHALLENGE

If you really want to have something to talk about on your first day at secondary school, do something different during the summer holidays. You don't have to travel far to experience something new. Try being a tourist where you live!

Calling all budding explorers

Take part in our Adventure Challenge this Saturday! All you need is a team of friends and a mobile phone. We'll set you the questions and then all you have to do is text in your answers. What are you waiting for? Enter your team today! Here are the first five questions to get you started ...

1 Everywhere has a spooky tale to tell – you just need to know where to look. Can you find some ghost stories to tell us?

2 We love to laugh. Take a picture of the strangest/funniest/most interesting statue you can find and text it to us.

3 We don't want the challenge to be too easy. Travel by three different types of transport and send us photos to prove it.

4 Go back in time. What is the oldest building where you live? We want to know.

5 Most places boast at least one famous person. Who's yours?

Getting started

- Gather a team of your most adventurous friends to take part.
- Text 07895432 to enter your team.
- Be at the town hall at 11a.m. on Saturday.
- You must get permission before you enter the challenge and a grown-up must accompany you.

Sending postcards (see idea 69) to your friends will help you with idea 60!

Top Tip!
Visit your local tourist information office for ideas of where to start on your challenge.

Why not do an adventure challenge for where you live?

62 Stay local
Explore your local tourist information office or website to see what's on.

63 Stay away
Stay at a friend's house and pretend it's a hotel. Be nice to the manager though!

64 Feel the beat
Visit a local event or festival to hear some new music or sample some new foods.

65 Make a mystery
Plan a mystery walking tour of the town for some friends to follow. Can you draw them a simple map too? Don't forget to get a grown-up to take part!

66 Chill out
Sit back and soak up the atmosphere like a real tourist! Have an ice cream or a picnic in the park.

67 Go camp-in!
Try camping indoors. It's warmer than outdoors and you still get to eat marshmallows!

68 Make it up
Make up your own tourist challenge. Challenge a friend to go to at least three places they've never been to before. Take a grown-up with you too.

69 Surprise your friends!
Send them each a postcard from your local area, saying 'Wish you were here!'

PERFECT A PARTY TRICK

Another thing to do in the summer holidays is perfect some party tricks. These will be your secret weapons, if there's an awkward silence in the playground at your new school.

Top Tip!
Juggling is tricky at first. Keep practising and you'll soon get it.

Throw it, catch it

Juggling always grabs a crowd's attention and pretty soon people will be queuing up to learn how it's done. However, juggling in the middle of a science lesson is probably a no-no!

How to juggle

1. First practise throwing one ball from one hand to another. Make sure each throw goes to the same height (up to your face) and wait for the ball to come to your other hand to catch it. Don't reach for it.

2. Next take two balls, one in each hand. Throw the red ball from one hand and when it reaches its highest point, throw the green ball up from the other hand so it flies *underneath* the first one.

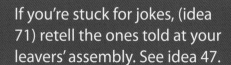

If you're stuck for jokes, (idea 71) retell the ones told at your leavers' assembly. See idea 47.

71 Keep them laughing
Learn ten new side-splittingly funny jokes.

72 Keep them guessing
Ask a grown-up to teach you a wicked new card trick.

73 String them along
Buy a yoyo and learn some yoyo skills – find out how to walk the dog, hop the fence and loop the loop!

74 Keep it up
Grab a football and practise your keepy-uppy skills.

75 Keep them talking ...
See how many languages you can learn to say 'Hi, my name is …' in.

76 Keep them listening ...
Find out something interesting about your new school. Is there a strange, spooky or funny story linked to it that will impress people when you tell them about it?

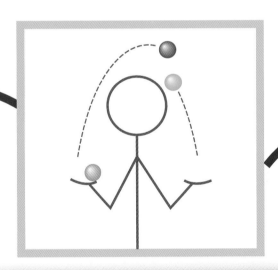

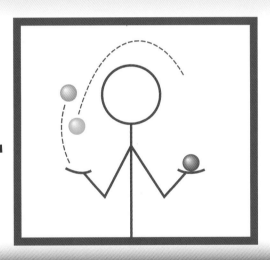

4. Then throw the blue ball from the starting hand over the green ball. Keep practising this until you can simply throw each ball just below the one before.

3. Now take two balls in one hand and one ball in the other. Throw the red ball from the hand with two balls first. When it is at its highest point, throw the green ball from the other hand.

How many balls do you need to juggle like this?

77 CUSTOMISE YOUR KIT

Crisp new shirt? Smart new trousers? Shiny shoes? It can mean only one thing – it's time for a new school uniform! Some people try to stretch the uniform code. Don't risk it. Schools can be super-strict about what you wear and, if you break the rules, you'll get into trouble.

Bags of personality

So how do you get the look without getting the detention? The answer is to stamp your personality on the other stuff you take to school with you – like your bag, lunch box or file. These things aren't usually part of any school dress code so you can express your personality by customising them in different ways.

FAST FACT
Modern school uniforms began in 18th century charity schools for the poor. Children wore uniforms because they were cheap and showed which school they went to.

Buy a file with a clear plastic cover and slide in a page of photos of you and your friends!

Find some fun wrapping paper to liven up your file. You could cover it with sticky-back plastic to stop it tearing.

STUDENTS FORCED TO TAKE NOTE

Teachers in the Isle of Wight have gone to unusual lengths to make sure students follow the school dress code, issuing sticky notes for uniform errors. Some students were made to wear the notes all day and feel teachers have gone too far. Staff, on the other hand, argue the notes were to stop the students continually being told off by members of staff on the lookout for incorrect uniforms. Whatever the truth, this is one school that takes their uniform very seriously.

Not all schools are as strict as this one.

78 Bag it
Collect or make badges to personalise your bag. You could use iron-on patches to make a fabric bag fabulous!

79 Focus on the extras
Look at the things you wear that aren't part of your uniform – like your coat, scarf and hat – and find ways to make these your own.

80 Think with your head!
Ask for a new haircut or wear a hairband or clips to make your hair a bit different.

81 Go vintage
Ask your sister/brother/neighbour to give you their old kit. Having kit that's a bit worn already will make you look effortlessly cool.

82 Get on the case
Decorate your pencil case. It'll brighten up even the dullest day!

83 Beautify your books
Cover your writing books with colourful wrapping paper. It'll make yours easy to spot in a pile on the teacher's desk.

Cut pictures out from old magazines to stick onto the file and then paint over them with PVA glue. Pick a theme, like sweets!

Top Tip!
Before you customise your file, ask your parents and check with someone who goes to your new school that it's OK to do it.

25

84 BE PREPARED!

Top Tip!
Assemble a survival kit to keep in your school bag. Include some cash and emergency telephone numbers.

It's the night before your first day at secondary school. How do you feel? Excited? Scared? Both? It's normal to feel a bit nervous. At a new school there will be new teachers, routines and people. All the new students will be feeling the same.

Sort it out

Most people feel better about their first day if they're prepared. By now you'll have your kit and uniform sorted so all you have to do is get ready to go.

Talk it out

When you're all prepared, it's time to sit back and relax. Still biting your nails and pacing the floor? Talk about it! It's amazing what a quick chat can do. If you've got an older friend, brother or sister, ask them how they felt the night before starting secondary school. They survived – and so will you!

Lay out your clothes so you can hop straight into them. Make sure you have everything clean and ready to wear, from your socks to your undies.

Don't forget to pack your newly customised kit from idea 77!

85 Check it out

Check out the times and the numbers of any buses you have to catch. This really helps if several different buses visit your stop.

86 Relax!

Take your mind off things the night before by watching a film or reading a good book.

87 Go to bed!

Get a good night's sleep – you'll find it easier to get up in the morning.

88 Get up early

Set your alarm 15 minutes early to give you extra time to get ready.

89 Plan it

Plan your route to school. You don't want to get lost on your first day!

90 Pal up

Agree to meet up with a friend in the morning and go to school together.

1. packed lunch!

2. pens, pencils and note pad!

3. pencil case!

5. apple!

6. change!

4. Bus timetable

Get a lunchbox ready or make sure you have cash to buy food. A rumbling tummy may not be the best way to get attention on your first day!

You can do it. The secret is preparation. Get everything ready the night before and you could be feeling this good too!

Pack your bag. Check school letters but you may only need a pen, pencil and a pad of paper.

FAST FACT

It's official! Breakfast really is the most important meal of the day. After a good night's sleep, you need breakfast to give your body energy. Without it, you won't be able to concentrate, remember or learn so well in the morning.

It's here at last – your first day at secondary school. You've got butterflies in your belly and you've burnt your toast. How will it go?

Breathe … Deeply …

No need to press the panic button. Every year thousands go through exactly the same thing and they all survive. So we thought the best people to give you advice were those who've just made the move themselves. Take a look at this web page for some great ideas …

Top Tip!
Most of the ideas are hidden on this page. Can you find nine things you could do to make your first day go well?

Help yourself to feel more relaxed about your first day by doing a bit of preparation beforehand – see idea 84.

EXTRA!

Tuesday, 24 August

HOW CAN WE SURVIVE THE FIRST DAY?

I can't believe the holidays are nearly over! Rubbish! Anyway, my friend Lucy and I are starting secondary school next week and we're really nervous. It's a massive school and we really don't know what to expect. We don't even know if we'll be in the same form! Has anyone got any advice on how we can survive the first day?

Posted by Anna10 at 1:47pm   9 comments

Real tips, real advice, real you!

HOME

HOMEWORK GETTING YOU DOWN?

BEING BULLIED?

WHICH CARTOON CHARACTER ARE YOU? TAKE TODAY'S QUIZ!

GAME ZONE

OTHER COOL STUFF

Ray says ...

Be brave. Talk to people and try to make new friends. You don't have to be like someone who's perfect. Just be yourself.

24 August at 5.47pm

Aisha says ...

Make sure you ask a teacher if you don't understand.

24 August at 7.47pm

Liz says ...

Always make sure the toilet door is locked and will stay locked!

25 August at 1.00pm

Kemal says ...

Stay organised and make sure you don't lose your homework, especially if you've already done it.

25 August at 6.00pm

Lily says ...

Always be early for your bus.

27 August at 11.15am

Jack says ...

Join lunchtime clubs as it makes it easier to make friends.

27 August at 12.30pm

Maddie says ...

If your school is really big, get a map from a teacher. Or ask people for directions.

29 August at 11.30am

Matt says ...

Make a couple of copies of your timetable, give one to your mum and colour code it.

30 August at 7.30pm

Harry says ...

Don't get stressed – everyone feels weird on the first day.

2 September at 2.28pm

Lots of people say your school days are the best days of your life. Why? What about all that homework?

More, more, more

Think about it. At secondary school there are more facilities and more activities than at primary school. That means more clubs to join, more to do and lots of new things to learn. At secondary school there are more people. That means more friends to make. What's not to like?

Well, there are probably always going to be things you might not like but hopefully the good will always outweigh the bad. So your final challenge is to do what it says at the top of the page – enjoy it!

I like school because I have made really good friends. We should feel privileged to go to school as people in poorer countries don't have this opportunity.

GLOSSARY

audition short performance someone gives to win a part in a show or play

autograph someone's signature

communicate way that people share information

director person in charge of a play or show

fossil fuel coal, oil or gas

gesture movement you make to show a particular meaning

paparazzi photographers who follow famous people around

posture position or way in which you hold your body

residential when you live somewhere else for a short time

stage name name an actor uses instead of their real name

time capsule container of things to tell people in the future how we live now

INDEX

autograph books 5
awards 14–15
body language 12–13
chatting and listening 13, 23
customising stuff 24–25
discos 17
exercise 10, 11
first day 28–29
food 11, 27
friends 5, 18–19, 27, 28–29, 30, 31
friendship bracelets 18–19
homework 11, 29
jokes 16, 23
leavers' day 16–17
local tourism 20–21
preparation 26–27
presents 17
school trips 6–7
shows and plays 8–9, 17
singing 5, 8–9, 17
smiling 13
sports 19
stress 10–11, 12
summer holidays 20–21
survival kit 26
survival tips 28–29
teachers 6, 7, 15, 17
time capsules 5
tricks 22–23
uniforms 24–25, 26
yearbooks 4–5